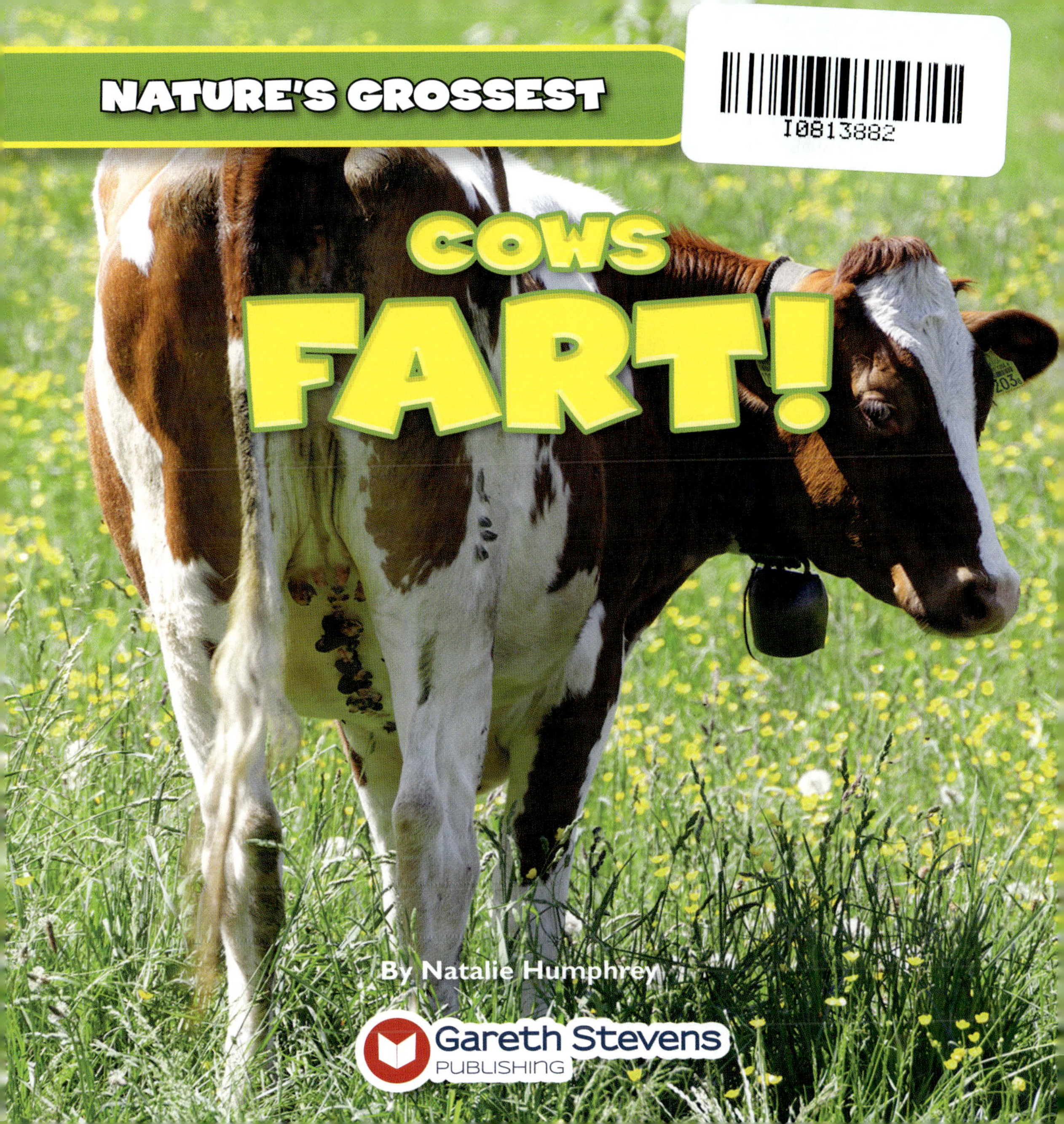
NATURE'S GROSSEST
I0813882
COWS
FART!
By Natalie Humphrey
Gareth Stevens
PUBLISHING

Please visit our website, www.garethstevens.com. For a free color catalog of all our high-quality books, call toll free 1-800-542-2595 or fax 1-877-542-2596.

Cataloging-in-Publication Data
Names: Humphrey, Natalie.
Title: Cows fart! / Natalie Humphrey.
Description: New York : Gareth Stevens Publishing, 2024. | Series: Nature's grossest | Includes glossary and index.
Identifiers: ISBN 9781538285626 (pbk.) | ISBN 9781538285633 (library bound) | ISBN 9781538285640 (ebook)
Subjects: LCSH: Cows–Behavior–Climatic factors–Juvenile literature | Flatulence–Juvenile literature. | Cows–Food–Juvenile literature.
Classification: LCC SF202.5 H86 2024 | DDC 636.2′142–dc23

Published in 2024 by
Gareth Stevens Publishing
2544 Clinton Street
Buffalo, NY 14224

Copyright © 2024 Gareth Stevens Publishing

Designer: Leslie Taylor
Editor: Natalie Humphrey

Photo credits: Series art (background) Oleksii Natykach/Shutterstock.com; cover Media Castle/Shutterstock.com; p. 5 Birkir Asgeirsson/Shutterstock.com; p. 7 Ruud Morijn Photographer/Shutterstock.com; p. 9 Roman Melnyk/Shutterstock.com; p. 11 Oaisu/Shutterstock.com; p. 13 Dajra/Shutterstock.com; p. 15 branislavpudar/Shutterstock.com; p. 17 Image Source Collection/Shutterstock.com; p. 19 Clara Bastian/Shutterstock.com; p. 21 Budimir Jevtic/Shutterstock.com.

All rights reserved. No part of this book may be reproduced in any form without permission in writing from the publisher, except by a reviewer.

Printed in the United States of America

CPSIA compliance information: Batch #CSGS24: For further information contact Gareth Stevens at 1-800-542-2595.

CONTENTS

Boldface words appear in the glossary.

Have You Ever Seen a Cow?

Cows are one of the most common farm animals. If you've seen a white animal with big black spots, chances are you've seen a cow! While cows look cute and cuddly, they do something gross a lot. They fart!

0517

Different Cows

There are many different types of cows. They are different colors and sizes. The most common type of cow in the United States is the Angus cow. Females are called "cows." Males are called "bulls."

On the Farm

Cows are mostly raised on two types of farms: dairy farms and meat farms. Dairy cows are raised to make milk for people to drink. Meat cows are raised to be eaten. There are around 92 million cows in the United States.

04301
04170

Hungry Cows

Cows eat a lot of different foods! They spend most of their time in a **pasture** where they can **graze**. Farmers sometimes give cows corn and oats. Cows also eat plant waste that would have gotten thrown away.

Gross Eaters

When a cow is eating, it doesn't chew its food just once! After a cow chews and swallows, that same food will come back up from the cow's **stomach** to its mouth. Then, the cow will chew its food again. Gross!

Four Stomachs

Cows have special stomachs that help them break down food other animals can't! A cow's stomach has four **chambers** that chewed plants go into. When a cow **digests** its food, the plants go back and forth through the chambers.

Gassy Grazers

When food breaks down in the cow's stomach, it creates a lot of gas. When gas builds up in a cow, just like when it builds up in a person, it has to come out. Cows not only fart—they burp!

Gross Gas

Cow burps and farts have the gas **methane** in them. The harder a cow needs to work to digest its food, the more methane it makes! Methane is one of the gases that scientists think may cause **climate change**.

Science to the Rescue!

Farmers have different ideas about how to stop their cows from farting! Some farmers have changed how their cows eat. Instead of just eating grass and plant waste, they give the cows foods that are easier to digest. This makes less gas!

GLOSSARY

chamber: A small room or space inside of something bigger.

climate change: Long-term change in Earth's climate, caused mainly by human activities such as burning oil and natural gas.

digest: To break down food inside the body so that the body can use it.

graze: To eat plants or grasses in a pasture.

methane: A common natural gas found on Earth.

pasture: Grass-covered land where animals eat.

stomach: The part of the body where digestion occurs.

FOR MORE INFORMATION

BOOKS

Boothroyd, Jennifer. *Baby Cows.* Minneapolis, MN: Bearport Publishing Company, 2022.

Pang, Ursula. *Dairy Farms.* Buffalo, NY: PowerKids Press, 2023.

WEBSITES

Britannica Kids
kids.britannica.com/kids/article/cattle/352928
Learn more interesting facts about how cattle live on a farm.

DK Find Out
www.dkfindout.com/us/animals-and-nature/domesticated-animals/cows/
Check out more photos of cows and learn how they live with other animals on farms.

Publisher's note to educators and parents: Our editors have carefully reviewed these websites to ensure that they are suitable for students. Many websites change frequently, however, and we cannot guarantee that a site's future contents will continue to meet our high standards of quality and educational value. Be advised that students should be closely supervised whenever they access the Internet.

INDEX